Ain' Love Grand

by
Kae Ling

the Peppertree Press
Sarasota, Florida

Kae Ling is the author-artist of many beloved books of prose and poetry.

Other titles by Kae Ling include—

Flutter-byes In My Hair

Resting My Eyes I See

Penny-Mom

Sunflower Harvest

Sealed With A Kiss

Dedicated to my guy~

I am

Grateful to be with he who sings and

Artfully happy just to sing along,

Resting forever in arms of love,

Young, once again.

Contents

Seeing Clearly

♥

When we
first meet
a potential
mate,
we can see
them quite
clearly for a
matter of

minutes. Then
our view is obscurred
by a rosie fog made up of
our own dreams, our fantasies,
our expectations and our hopes.

After those first few minutes,
we never see the real face
of our beloved again.
sigh

A Distant Caress

♥

Eyes open to a fine line
  of trees off in the distance
    as I lay there on ground hard
     and soft.
       Gentle breeze moves small curls
        and I stroke the grasses,
         feeling the life in each blade.
        Oh, for a camera to take
         in this view and preserve
          the memory of my ground!
         The mound I caress has
           the scent of sunshine and smiles.
         There is life here
           and the rumbling of distant
           thunder tickles my ear as
            you say my name.

A Perfect Match

♥

Some are silly
    and not so smart.
Some are plain,
    but still art.
Some are too shy,
    too bold,
        too young,
            and way too old.
Some make you laugh,
    cry,
        cringe,
    or sigh.
But a perfect match
    oh Lord, I see,
        a perfect match
            you made for me!

All Hope Is Not Lost

♥

Amidst the celebration
of one so dear,
birthday wishes and
the clanking of dishes,
I stole a moment to
see through foggy windows.
Well wishers have come from afar
to participate.
The yellow flowers
"scent" the invitation
to friends and they all arrived!
Honey Bees wishing
my Honey a
very happy birthday and
szzzpreading the pollen
love notezzzz to everyone
that all hope izzz "<u>not</u>" lozzzzt!

Alone

Alone I am and alone I'll stay

waiting for some far away

magical being to come to me.

Someone who was meant to be

mine and mine alone.

Ahhh, there you are.

Bear Afternoon

♥

In the morning,
    when the doves sing,
        the bugs buzz
            so loud, my ears ring.
I look forward to
    the bear's afternoon
        delights,
            a snooze, a hug,
                snuggle and cuddle.
Then the phrase
    I've grown to expect,
        and anticipate....
* I respond *

Beginnings

♥

Where are the beginnings?
I've seen the endings
    and the in-betweens.
There was a beginning,
    somewhere.
Now, lost among memories
    I wanted, but were not mine.
A proper beginning,
    middle and ending,
      is the way a story goes,
        without interruptions,
          intermissions or abrupt
          bombings.
When will the time be right?
Where are all my beginnings?

Oh, there you are.

Caterpillar

♥

Little fuzzy caterpillar
    with your clicky feet
    tickle my forehead
    as you travel on your rounds;
    tickle, smack, smack, tickle.
I can hardly stand it, but move?
Not I! I love your little
    kisses as on your rounds you go
    across my forehead,
    down my cheek,
    over my shoulder
    as you leave my arm
    and travel back to
    mossy acre.
We watch the sun come up
    together.
One last glance into
    each other's eyes and
    the day begins.
* Love you *,
    my fuzzy caterpillar.

Copper Dragonflies

♥

Copper glistening in the sun
    dancing here and there,
        floating on waves and breezes,
            caught my eye as I dreamed
                in the noonday sun.

Dragonflies galore
    came to visit for awhile.
Copper flicks as sunlight licks
    pristine wings,
    here, in my noonday sun.

My Favorite Times

♥

My favorite times

    are spent with you,

        while the day blinks

            and kisses Luna adieu.

First Time

♥

The first time I heard
    it said, I thought I
    heard it wrong
What? says I.
The bear whispers in my ear
    a phrase so soft and low.
So embarassed, so hot,
    I was in shock!
* a private phrase *
    * just for me *
** ahhh ** love.

The Football Player and The Poet

♥

The football player,
    the poet,
    and a new beginning.
A hopeful heart
    at the last of their years
    till God sees fit
    to pull them apart.

The football player,
    a quarterback,
    swore he'd never, ever
    do it again.
He met a poet,
    an old familiar face
    and somewhere he found grace.
She came to him
    with timid open arms
    "I hope" is her fav to say.
He took her in lock, stock, and barrel.
He kept her safe and
    gave her his all
    and she tried not to worry.
She contemplates the future and now,
    writes of love...

My Green Acre

♥

The sun warms my acre.
My moss filled bed is
    where I lay my head
    every chance I get.
It is mine.
I snuggle deeper
    down and caress the
    thick carpet with fingers
    splayed - I played
    with the softer patch curling
    it between my thumb and forefinger.
Glorious, softness, where the
    firmness of the earth and gentleness
    of the breeze caress my back
    meets spiced limbs.
The smell intoxicates
    and I am happy
    in my green acre.

I Looked Up

♥

I looked up
into your face,
open, calm and eager.
Lashes like an artist's
favorite brush.
Eyes sparkle with
amusement and energy.
* Yes *

$\mathcal{I}$ wait

♥

This weight on my chest
    tightens as I lay to rest.
The loving caress of the boa turns
    and wraps me, embracing
    with strength I knew not.
Comforting though it may be,
    I hold off to see,
    what this weight is on my chest.
The smell of earth fills me
    with desire for this weight on my chest.
Dampness, as I sink deeper,
    drenches me and the grass
    beneath moves to the hush
    of this weight on my chest.
I embrace it and my breath eases
    out in a rush - short bursts of haaahh...
I open my eyes as cool clean air comes
    back to refresh.
Wishing again to feel this weight
    on my chest
              * I wait *

In Wee Hours

♥

I sleep with bear
    and bear sleeps with me.
Soundly snoring
    comforts this aloneness
    in wee hours,
        in wee hours.
The rise and fall
    this chest of fur,
    I sleep with bear
    and bear sleeps with me.
Muse wakes me
    and we talk awhile
    rousting me
    with the usual visual.
Times of tears,
    times of joy,
    some with smiles,
    some with years,
    bypass and wave.
Bear hugs,
    wrap around me,
    and soundly paws my muse
    sending Muse to outerspace,
    in wee hours,
        in wee hours.

In Your Arms

At first it was a

    mountain, a hill

    to look over and around.

I counted the blades

    of grass and the way

    some shined in the sun.

I could hear the beat

    and feel the heat as

    I pressed into the

    musky scented mound,

    giving and ungiving

    at the same time.

Last Thoughts of Dispair

Memories bubble to the surface,
    popping, exploding into
    lights, threatening the
    glow of your love.
Despair dissolved on my skin
    like grease finally melting,
    grudgingly sliding
    down my back,
    over my buttocks,
    around my thighs,
    through my toes
    and into the earth below,
    gone.

Life Sings

♥

Fingers splayed among
    grey hair
    soft and so curly
    barely felt there.
Skin taut with anxiousness
    awaiting sweet release
    utter sounds of praise
    wanting only to please.
The sun is up,
    a day begun
    in quiet wonder
    and life sings once again.
Rumbling tones
    under rambling thumbs,
    questioning love proclaimed.
In answer, I reply,
    and life sings once again.

Love Quest

♥

In my quest to find love,
     I forgot to bring myself.
To please,
     to bend as a willow
     with the wind,
     to be what all expect,
     and yet....
Myself is afraid
     but a brave front
     is there in control.
I put it on as a coat
     to shield me from the cold,
     to protect and to hold
     the innert thing I call a heart.
Sleep came knocking and I
     ignored it and plodded onward.

Knock, knock, it bid me follow.
I did not answer and
        as if on cue, there arrived
        at the door of my conscience,
        myself, angry, defiant,
        almost hysterical, demanding
        to know what I thought
        I was doing on my own,
        alone, on my quest
        to find love.
I closed the door on myself
        content at last, finding love,
        while love found me.

Love

I asked love this morning,
  "where do you hide?"

Love answered,
  "here, in the warmth of lips."

I looked deeply into the soul
  and found the true nature of the heart.

Man

♥

I wonder how much we know
about the story and how it goes.
What do we really understand
and think about the human man.
Clark Kent, he ain't
and Simon Templer ain't no saint.
So who is that man of mine,
when he's mean and when he's kind?
What lies beyond my eyes,
could be kisses and lots of sighs.
Ah, yes, my man!
He is the man in my dreams
not whom everyone sees,
but the one I prayed for on my knees.

Mate

♥

When your mate is
        far away,
                the sun doesn't shine
                    the same old way.
There are friends and family abound
            but the one I seek
                    can't be found.
Miss you, mate.

Murmur - Among Strangers

A heart murmur, the doc
    wants to take a look.
He doesn't know that
    your heart murmurs to mine.
An echo of your heart today
    they will take.
My heart will echo back -
    "I wait."
Half hour to one hour
    here, among strangers,
    I watch as the time
    ticks away.
Your face, as you went
    through the door,
    said I'll be right back,
    here, with you.
I watched your face for
    signs of worry or care,
    you showed no fear
    only concern for me
    here, among strangers.

And so I'll sit and patiently
wait for you
to come back to me
10:30....11:45....
here, among strangers.

Come Away My Beloved

When you ache,
>> I will wash away the years,
>> I will carress you with my tears.

When you thirst,
>> I will lead you to water,
>> I will hold your hand.

Lord, bless this one
>> who has soothed
>> my troubles
>> and caressed me
>> with words of
>> kindness and gentleness,
>> speaking haltingly and
>> is slow to anger.

He hears Your call.

He took me out of loneliness
>> into togetherness and
>> smoothed my troubled brow.

I gave to him all I
>> have and pray keep him
>> from all harm.

When this mortal coil
        fails and all is looking dim,
        I pray to You to
        give him your light
        and welcome him in.
Leave me or take me too
        because you know with
        him I'll ask to go.

My Gary Gary

Through my years
>>I've never known anyone
>>with your qualities.
First is patience,
>>of which you gave to me
>>freely and I've watched you
>>give to all you meet.
Next, is laughter
>>of which, without it,
>>there would be no sun.
The best is your love,
>>there is no end to it,
>>with me or our children.
Gary Gary,
>>you double my pleasure,
>>double my fun,
>>my Gary Gary.

My Valentine Roses

A perfect rose - I longed.

Received twelve, one perfect dozen.

A true love - I longed.

All this, resting against the
palm of His hand.

The breath of babes and eucalyptus
ascend to the Heavens in thanks.

Petals curving outward
then curling under to reveal
petticoats of reds and yellows.

The look of love so true.

Valentine, * I love you *.

No Fear

♥

Flowers grow here.
I see them every day.
Small red, orange
    in all hues of love.
Trees keep your smile safe
    from that which would crush.
Leaves shade the yes in your eyes
    from tears that threaten.
Have no fear...
    Hush ...
        I love you dear....

Oh, Man!

♥

The way we lean into each other.
How soft your lips are!
When your eyes close,
will your perfect jade green
tangle with my forever blue,
turning everything to aquamarine?
My hands gravitate to the
sides of your face,
my thumb lightly brushes
your cheek as I lose my breath
and my heart settles into your chest...
Universal magic washes away the need
for keeping track of time.
Have we been here for moments or decades?
Centuries could pass with your
eyes flashing at me -
passion deep within.
Oh, man!

Peace

There is sadness in his eyes
      so green and true.
There's a sadness in
      my land, oh Lord,
      a heaviness in my steps.
If you see fit to take him home,
      please let the arrow slip and
      find me as well.
Not to be, is my request,
      for his sadness I cannot bear.

Rain Dance

Oh, to be in love
on a rainy night!
The bush says "GO!"
and my heart takes flight.
Out of the open window it flees
into the air and rain to seize
a moment or two,
in time to please
this old soul.
To dance in the rain
with Love is my goal.

Rainbows

Wild grass pulled
    as sweat tried to cool.
Poison for the choking weeds,
    we watered and pruned,
    clipped and snipped,
    loaded and hauled.
The sun chased us inside
    as the sweat cooled tiredness.
Mulch applied once again
    and all is well
    on the mighty ranch.
Soon, the hedges will reach their
    height and the cycle
    will start over.
Thunder warns and
    lightning shows the way.
I look forward to the rainbows.

Rock

♥

To rock this child
    who isn't mine
        from the body of my beloved.
To hold this babe
    so helpless and pure...
Pressed into my arms,
    protected from harm,
        will only know love from me.

Sinking

♥

I was sinking in waters blue
     struggling against each new hue,
    with waves tossing to and fro.
Hands, salty from age,
       held me there to see
           all the things it hid from me.
Now, safe am I
     riding the tides.

Stillness

I feel a stillness here.
Can a place have memories
        or a face?
I think it can.
I feel a stillness here,
        a waiting, of sorts.
A place where things have died,
        the smells mingle of old wood,
        dust, and earth,
        beneath and floating up.
This place leans
        to give a better view from
        a too small window.
The leaves outside have
        turned up their noses
        to await love which
        God is about to give.

Surf

Surf wave after wave,
      life's surges and ebbs.
The lilt of the voice echoes against the walls
      of my heart aching to be free.
Around and around the lilting goes until
      I think I'll lose my sanity.
Why does it not free itself ?
Surely, it knows its way out.
The walls of my heart are battered
      and bruised from the song.
Still, my heart holds it,
      for I could not bear never to hear it again.
The lilt with the "come with me"
      yearning only love can satisfy.

Swish

♥

You said...

    I heard...

I said...

    You heard ...

The pendulum is moved to tears

    as it hears the sweetness of years

      go by...

Swish... swish...

    from left to right,

      from dark to light,

swish... swish...

* love *

The Dress

♥

A touch of ivory
    a touch of peach
    and a touch of pearls,
    and for me,
    some of each.
This, once upon a time,
    are what I dreamed
    when youth was mine,
    hanging there together
    in the closet of my mind.

The Look

♥

I saw the look, ah, the look;
     head up, wind-blown hair,
     dark green, smiling eyes,
     ah, the look ...
Oh, for that look
     twas it for me?
     the look...

It's been awhile
     and memory fails me
     at times,
     but this is not one of them.

Memories attack my senses
     and my heart skips a beat,
     * ahh *, for that look ....

The Soft Goodbye

♥

Is there really a soft goodbye?
"Yes, my dear", the wind sighed.
The flutes call and the drum
beats out my steps while
violins give lift to my wings,
hidden for so long.
"The die has been cast", a lone
viola sings.
The belly stirs a deepness of longing
of a question that will never be asked.
* sigh *

This rose

    tells me I am alone.

She tells me of future

    mistakes

        and whispers of

            longing to be loved.

Ahh,

        there you are. . . .

This Small Bird

♥

What would you give up to achieve

oneness with love?

What would you do for love?

Caressing my head with his

breath and dancing

to the music of life,

he holds and guides with

the strength of his arms.

Pressing me to him,

I rest in his embrace.

Promises kept....

This small bird will nest.

To Know You Better

♥

I looked at the yearbook,

    looked at the albums,

    and looked deep into your eyes,

    to know you better.

I looked at your family,

    listened to the stories,

    and watched your reactions,

    to know you better.

We watched programs you like,

    ride around town,

    eat in restaurants,

    went to the beach,

    ate with family,

    and played cards,

    to know you better.

Time very well spent,

    to know you better.

Yearning

The grey tiger with eyes of deep dark green,
sparks of brown glisten therein,
has departed and gone on its way.
Left behind is the scent on my pillow
of a yearning for Spring,
for things that might have been.

Called Home

There was love in this place
   at one time young. Now,
   God has called us home.
I will be my younger self
   as I sit to wait under yonder tree.
I ponder how the meeting will be
 and pray you will remember me.
This one to you is true
   this one whose eyes are blue,
   not the perfect body,
   not the perfect hair,
   but with almost perfect love,
   the one who'll always care. * sigh *
You will see me sitting there as
   time has brought us for the last mile,
   to walk on together with love in between
   hand in hand we'll talk, remembering.
* sigh *
God, at last, has called us home.

He Cares

The peace of tomorrow is in the shadow of
    today's setting sun,
      where the gold and purples
      blend to mirror my love's eyes.
Thundering just below the surface,
    promising passion unknown before,
    he held my hand centuries ago and
    the fire has never left.
When he returns for me,
    as promised, I will be but the
        mist that will surround him wherever
          he should go and I will ache no more
          satisfied within, he cares.

The Key

♥

The key
to
immortality:

Date
a
poet!

Honey

When there's a rumble deep, I love.
When eyes of green laugh, I love.

These small thoughts and poems are for you,
    my love.
He stands there with his toe in the sand, hands
in his pockets,
    hair askew, looking up through lashes
    with eyes twinkling,
        "Aw shucks."

CPSIA information can be obtained
at www.ICGtesting.com
Printed in the USA
FFOW03n0645190518
46678136-48761FF